Brothers and Sisters

Karl König

Brothers and Sisters

The Order of Birth in the Family

Floris Books

First published in 1958, fourth edition 1963
Reprinted in 2004

© 1958, 1963 Rudolf Steiner Publications Inc, New York

British Library CIP Data available

ISBN 0-86315-446-8

Printed in Great Britain
by The Bath Press, Bath

Contents

Foreword

In this book, a recognized classic, Karl König asks the always intriguing question: Does birth order influence our way of life, motivation and character? His findings suggest that these are not influenced by our birth order in a simple and direct way. He proposes a theory of 'family constellations' to explain how our place within our family shapes the way we make social contact with others.

König's book was written in 1963. Naturally, some of the language and examples he has chosen appear dated now. Some readers may dislike his use of the male gender as his reference point, but this was the common language of the time. Putting aside these anachronisms, we must acknowledge that König was a pioneer. His analysis builds on earlier research — pointing out how little was known at the time and affirming that, in certain circumstances, birth order can be important for the character of the developing child. König keeps in mind inherent individual differences and does not lose sight of other important factors, such as gender and socio-cultural environment. His fascinating study set down a solid foundation for future understanding.

König uses analogy, case studies, related research and his own investigations to explore and illustrate commonalities in the characteristics and achievements of only children, and first-, second- and third-born children. Complex relationships between siblings born into different 'family constellations' are not forgotten, and König identifies patterns that appear to be repeated with additional children. Furthermore, he understands the importance of communication and companionship, and provides an insight into how birth order can influence an individual's aptitude for these.

König is realistic about the range of topics that should be taken into account when considering how birth order may shape a child's ability to form relationships, and how this can affect self-esteem, intelligence and motivation beyond childhood. His thoughtful book highlights a wide variety of issues that are still important for birth order researchers today, and of abiding interest to parents.

Niki Powers, MA, MSc

Colwyn Trevarthen
Professor (Emeritus) of Child
Psychology and Psychobiology

Department of Psychology
The University of Edinburgh

Introduction

The original title of this little book was: 'The Order of Birth in the Family Constellation.' As this is rather cumbersome and not fully understandable to the general reader, we decided to alter it and just to say 'Brothers and Sisters', because it deals with the relationship between brothers and sisters and with the problems of the order of birth. Is there any significance in the fact of being a first-, second- or third-born child? Does this order influence our way of life as well as our motivations and our character?

We are not the first to ask this question. It is generally known that an only child — growing up without the influence of other brothers and sisters — is often peculiar in his behaviour and usually rather immature in his social conduct. It is not too difficult to understand the special position of such a lonely bird.

But should it matter whether I am born as first, second or third child? Can there be any significance in such a chance-arrangement? Some psychologists — like Alfred Alder and others — have attributed special traits of character to first- and second-born children. More recent investigations have shown that first-born people have stronger neurotic tendencies compared with their brothers or sisters.

Margarete Lautis — after a follow up study among the families of former Harvard students — writes:

> The eldest child is adult-orientated. He is more likely to be serious, sensitive (that is, his feelings are hurt easily and he does not need much punishment) conscientious, 'good', fond of books, or fond of doing things with adults.
> He may either be a mama's child and shy, even fearful, or he may be self-reliant, independent and undemonstrative ... In one case the child has to keep close to an adult and be

directed by him or her. In the other case he imitates the adult and becomes a small facsimile of one.

The second child is not so anxious to get adult approval; in this sense he is tougher. He is likely to be either placid, easy going, friendly, cheerful, easy to take care of (although he makes no special effort to please) or else stubborn, rebellious, independent (or apparently so) and able to take a lot of punishment. What these two have in common is relative insensitivity to adult scolding and relative isolation from adults.[1]

In this rather striking characteristic of the difference between first- and second-born children we find some special psychological attributes which are representative for each group. Is this not in itself a significant discovery?

More recently The Workers Educational Association in London has encouraged a field-study on 'the influence of the order of birth upon the educational opportunities and leisure pursuits of 7000 school children.'[2] In the 'Summary' of her investigation, *Mary Stewart* states:

It was found that the elder of two were more successful than the younger of two and the eldest of three or more were more successful than the youngest of three or more children in obtaining Grammar school places.'

Remaining at school beyond the statutory leaving age was more common among first-born than among last-born children. In Grammar schools, the proportion of elder and eldest children increased from 34% of those under fifteen years of age to 43% of the pupils of sixteen years and over; the proportion of younger and youngest children decreased over the same period from 29% to 20%.

Membership of the uniformed organizations (Scouts, Guides, Boys' and Girls' Brigade) was larger among elder and eldest than among youngest children.

The elder of two went less often and the youngest of three or more children, more often to the cinema than those in other family positions.

In Modern schools, pursuits demanding individual efforts were named more often as favourite activities by the elder of two and less often by the youngest of three or more children than by those in other family positions.

These findings reveal again some significant differences between first- and later-born children. It would, however, be wrong to conclude that a first-born child is more intelligent than his siblings. This is not the case! Extensive investigations among children and adults have shown that there is no marked difference in the IQ (intelligence quotient) between first- and later-born children.

Mary Stewart comes to the same conclusion. She points out that 'In State Schools, last-born children tend to take less advantage of their opportunities than first-born' and she clearly adds: 'Last-born children are not by virtue of their position less intelligent than the first-born. They may, however, have less self-confidence and fewer incentives to make maximum use of their abilities'.

There can be no doubt that special traits of character and mental make-up are found in children and adults who belong to the different ranks in the order of birth. It is much more difficult to state with some clarity as to where these differences lie. They seem to belong more to the sphere of the emotional life and the structure of the personality than to the realm of intelligence and general ability.

The first-born person is usually much more attached to his parents than the rest of his brothers and sisters. He tries especially hard to adhere to the adult world or to transform himself into a little adult. He shows more zeal, perseverance and drive than his siblings. Thus he loses the carefree mood of childhood much too soon. Also during the later years the first-born remains a hard worker. He tries to push on in his career and, if possible, to reach the top of the tree.

The second-born are quite different. They usually take things much easier and are, therefore, less strict and strained. They try to make the best out of life and like to enjoy it as much as possible. For the second-born life is not only a task which has to be managed; it is much more an opportunity for gaining pleasure, wonder and beauty.

The third-born have again a different character. They usually are the 'odd man out'. They do not mix easily with others, are restrained, self-conscious and often rather difficult to get on with. But they have other qualities. Their mind reaches high up and sometimes they are visionaries or leaders.

Such differences can be found if an all-round study of first-, second- and third-born people is made. But where do these differences lie? They are not just variations in the make up of character and mind; they reach much deeper into the subtle structure of the whole of the personality.

What is the real difference which we meet in the ranks of birth? We will find an answer only if we try to study the deeper motives which fundamentally influence a person when meeting the world. The encounter between human beings and their whole environment — people and weather and demands and opportunities and destiny and everything which is not they themselves — is basically determined by his rank in the order of birth.

The *first-born* attempts to conquer the world.

The *second-born* tries to live in harmony with the world.

The *third-born* is inclined to escape the direct meeting with the world.

The fourth, fifth and sixth child repeat the basic trends of a first, second and third-born and so do the seventh, eighth and ninth, and so on. The later children, which follow the third, display the same fundamental characteristics as the three first ones. So the ranks of birth have to be counted in the following way:

	First-born	Second-born	Third-born
Rank of Birth	1st	2nd	3rd
	4th	5th	6th
	7th	8th	and so on

The three fundamental traits which determine the relation between the individual and the world are characteristics for the three ranks of birth. They influence our life in a similar way as our sex determines our character. Whether we are male or female reaches deep down into the formation of our character and into the shape of our personality. To recognize this as clearly as possible is a task for our age. If it is properly understood it will help parents and teachers to understand much better their children and pupils and to comprehend the underlying motives of their reactive behaviour.

The ranks of birth imprint their traits on each one of us. From birth onwards we are under the yoke of this great law and it will be the task of the following pages to explain in some detail the various characteristics of first-, second- and third-born people. As I said already, this law determines our relation to our environment in a similarly fundamental way as does our sex. A man has different forms of behaviour than a woman. From early infancy we are modelled by being either male or female. We are equally modelled and destined by our rank of birth.

Much too little attention has been paid to this great rune so far. May this thesis help to make it better known so that its realization in turn will help to build a better world!

The Only Child

I

There are so many forces, powers and circumstances that determine the existence of a human being that to unravel the tremendously complicated skein and to recognize the different threads is very difficult. There are certain qualities that are inborn and the individuality is destined by them. Our temperaments, for instance, whether we are phlegmatic or choleric, sanguine or melancholic, develop out of the depths of our being and are by no means determined by our environment. Many of the talents and inclinations we bring with us wake up from the deepest and innermost recesses of our unconscious being.

On the other hand there are qualities determined by the environment of the earliest days of our childhood. During the first year of life, every baby learns to utter and lisp and coo every conceivable vowel and consonant. Later, however, by imitating the language spoken in its surroundings, it learns its special mother-tongue, a language permeated by all the special hues and inflexions characteristic of the small environment of the growing child. By means of imitation, every child speaks the dialect of its surroundings.

Yet, not only the language is imitated: every district, every village, every county has its own gestures besides specific dialect. A man from Birmingham moves his hands slightly differently from a Glaswegian. The nod of the head acknowledging a Good Morning is as indicative of an Aberdonian as it is different anywhere else. Even the various districts of the larger towns such as London, Vienna or Berlin are clearly distinguishable by dialect, gesture and the manner in which people dress and carry themselves.

These are rather extreme examples, but they make us realize how manifold are the innate powers and the external influences that ultimately shape and mould our personality. Among these numerous and determinating factors is one that usually escapes our attention although it is one of the greatest importance. It is a factor that permeates a large part of our social life and behaviour.

This factor is the place of birth that every child assumes in his own family; whether he is an only child or one among several brothers and sisters; whether he is a single boy among a flock of sisters or a girl in a horde of brothers. It is of importance for the whole life of a man whether he was the first, second or third child, whether he was an older boy when smaller brothers and sisters came along after him, or whether he himself was the last one with two or three brothers and sisters already grown up whilst he was still a toddler. Innumerable possibilities exist here and have a deep influence on human life.

If we try to recognize the kind of qualities created by the family-constellation of the growing child, we do not find the answers easily. Several investigations have been carried out to elucidate certain common features in first, second or third children, but very few binding discoveries were made. One of these studies says that many investigations 'have shown that the first-born are on the average smaller and lighter at birth than later-born in the same families. They include more prematures and more cases of abnormal confinement. Studies of later health and physical development have not yet yielded consistent results.'[3]

Rather extensive investigations of the different levels of intelligence in the first and later-born children have led to negative findings. No conspicuous differences could be evaluated.

Yet differences exist, and a trained observer is often able to say whether a person is first-born or not. Also, an only child shows peculiar qualities in certain fields of its general make-up. Can we point to any specific sphere where these differences occur? Can we recognize the field where these characteristic qualities are to be found?

It becomes more and more obvious to me that neither the

grade of intelligence nor the talents and instincts, the temperament and the character of person are determined by his family-constellation. These qualities belong almost entirely to his own personality. They are partly determined by heredity, they are also the result of pre-earthly experiences gone through by every human being.

The family-constellation, however, shapes the *social* behaviour of man. It determines the way he reacts to other people; how he is able to make friends or not, the way he finds companionship and community with others. Even the choice of a husband or wife is deeply influenced by the facts of the family-constellation.

All these social patterns are guided and formed out by the use of the fundamental forces that establish the relations of men to one another: the powers of contact. But before going further in our deliberations, let us ask: What is this human contact? What are the forces in man to which we may ascribe the special powers that enable us to meet other people? Is it at all possible to define and to describe them?

II

There is hardly a chapter in modern psychology so greatly neglected as the one on human contact, that very special quality upon which our social life mainly depends. We all know the type of person who makes easy contact with any sort of his fellow-men. When he enters a room where others are gathered, he will soon be the centre of the party. People flock around him because they feel safe and warm in his vicinity. There is a friendly word for everyone, a smile, an encouraging look, a hearty handshake.

Others, however, have the greatest difficulty in meeting their fellow-men and in establishing contact with them. They are shy, retired, and only under the greatest strain are they able to enter into a good talk. Between these two types there are many transitional stages that determine the social behaviour of every individual.

In pathological conditions, the contact-qualities can unfold to the extreme or can fail almost completely. There are children, for instance, who are so eager to make contact with others that they are unable to restrain themselves from embracing any person who comes their way. They overflow in their sympathies and make no distinction in their object of contact. On the other hand, there are children and adult people who are more or less entirely unable to contact or approach others. They need not be self-centred, but the bridge between them and their social environment is missing. Some are completely enclosed in their own world, others establish superficial verbal contact without really meeting the other person. There are children who are unable to draw near to other children and therefore forego the possibility of common games and common experiences in every field of life.

In Jung's psychology, these two types are described as *extroverted* and *introverted* personalities.

> The extrovert thinks, feels and acts in reference to the object; he displaces his interest from the subject out upon the object, he orientates himself predominantly by what lies outside him. With the introvert, the subject is the starting-point of his orientation and the object is accorded a most secondary, indirect value. This type of man draws back at first in a given situation, as if with an unvoiced 'No,' and only then follows his real reaction.[4] And Jung himself is of the opinion that introversion or extroversion, as a typical attitude, means an essential bias which conditions the whole psychic process, establishes the habitual reactions, and thus determines not only the style of behaviour, but also the nature of subjective experience.[5]

There is hardly any doubt that these two fundamental types of behaviour in all their manifold shades and grades have a great deal to do with the social contact of every human being. They determine the connection between the human subject and the objects around him. But we do not mean to identify these very small forms of behaviour with actual human contact, because the introversion or extroversion shows nothing else but the direction of the individual towards his environment. It describes the ability or inability of the Ego to meet the other personality. But the act of meeting, the factual contact, is not as yet described when we speak of introverted or extroverted people.

There is no human being who does not have an element of introversion as well as extroversion in the make-up of his psyche. Only the grading and mixture vary in each personality, so that one person may have strong extrovert tendencies and therefore appear as an extrovert. But he has a good amount of introvert qualities, too, which can be quite well established, although they may appear to be overpowered by the extrovert forces. In the same way, an introvert person has a certain amount of extroversion which he manifests at special moments and in special situations.

Man is always and in every possible respect a being consisting of two opposing forces. Such polar opposite powers determine and hold each other at bay. This is also the case with the two polarities that express themselves in extroversion and introversion.

Where do these two tendencies originate? Is there a region in the whole realm of the human psyche that is either introvert or extrovert? Or is it the personality itself in its twofold aspect?

It does not seem to be too difficult to give an answer to this question. A simple introspection might help us to understand this problem. When, for instance, we contemplate a difficult idea or when we try to solve a complicated problem, we concentrate our thoughts and rather neglect our surroundings. We withdraw into the realm of ideas and try to do nothing else but to 'collect our thoughts.' We even close our eyes and sometimes bury our head in our hands, indicating an introvert attitude.

Quite different is our behaviour when we are engaged in activities connected to our will-power. Here we forget ourselves and are deeply engrossed in the object of our activity. Whether we lay bricks or dig a plot of earth, whether we make a pair of shoes or plough up a field, every work of this and every other kind demands of a person that he identify himself with the object. A workman who does not love his piece of work will hardly be able to do his job in a perfect way. In every activity of will that we perform, we have to be extrovert in order to do it well.

And now we recognize the fact that the source of introversion lies in the sphere of thinking, whereas all extroversion springs from the region of the will. Both the introvert as well as the extrovert powers are needed in every human being because we are *thinkers* as much as we are *doers*.

If a man is too intellectual, he will have greater difficulty in establishing social contact than he who is of the more active type. The latter has less inhibitions in meeting another person directly. The thinker will be hesitant and more on the defensive when trying to contact others.

Here lies the fountainhead of the two qualities that determine the direction of all human contact. But what region is the source of the contact itself? Let us try again to exercise some introspection. Everything that surrounds us, be it a part of nature or man-made, has a special connection to us. We do not only observe it and think about it; we do not only neglect it or long for it. As soon as we meet an object, we invest it with a mantle of like or dislike. And no one should think that he is so objective as to experience neither sympathy nor antipathy when encountering an object. With every thing and every person, we experience an immediate sensation that arises from the depths of our being. We feel it also with animals, flowers and plants, with stones and crystals. Sound, noise, colour and shadow, smell and taste — everything around us kindles an immediate emotional contact in us.

The secret of every contact-situation is that the bond between the individual and the object is an emotional one. It is in the sphere of *feeling* that we meet the surrounding world and do so with either sympathy or antipathy. And often what we experience is not simple like or dislike. There are different shades of so-called ambivalent feelings; we may like and dislike the same object at the same time.

Our sympathies are always connected with extroversion and our antipathies with introversion; extroversion is the direction of sympathy, introversion of antipathy. Thus we must recognize that both dislike as well as like are the wings of contact between the individual and the world. We meet the surroundings in either way. Only the direction is a different one, and too much sympathy is as difficult and as unbearable as is too much antipathy.

Man's social powers lie in the sphere of his emotions. He reaches out with his sympathetic forces, and draws back with the antipathetic ones. It is a kind of breathing process; an exhaling in sympathy and an inhaling in antipathy. This is the human contact-situation. To have very little or no contact at all does not mean to have a great deal of antipathy; it means to have neither likes nor dislikes but a very small amount of emotional ability.

It is in the sphere of emotional life and feeling where man displays his contact with the surrounding world. He meets his environment in antipathy as well as in sympathy. Love and hatred, extroversion and introversion, are elements necessary as tools for his social existence. In childhood he learns to exercise these powers.

III

Let us again return to that peculiar factor determined by the family-constellation during childhood. How does it influence our social contact, this peculiar sphere of our emotional life? What bearing can the family-situation have on the unfolding of our feelings? Are our likes and dislikes determined by the number of brothers and sisters among whom we grow up?

In order not to make things too complicated, we shall first discuss a very special constellation: that of the Only Child — this strange specimen of man who grows up under the direct wings of his parents, being their one and all. The latter's life is centred around this only child whose existence is fixed to mother and father. It is a rather special situation and we might be able to gain some understanding for its specific nature.

Just recently an English poet published his childhood memories and gave to his book the title: *The Only Child*.[6] The frontispiece shows the photograph of a little boy standing in an open doorway and looking out into the world. His gaze goes far into the distance, into the nowhere. An air of remoteness lies around this little figure who wears trousers and a woollen jumper, crumpled stockings and old sandals. Here the true image of an only child is perfectly revealed. The only child stands in the doorway, he is neither in nor out, he is almost always at the threshold. Behind him is the haven of his nest, before him lies the glory of the world. But he is neither here nor there. He is unable to enjoy the warmth of his nest nor does he dare to make the jump into the fullness of life. He remains a figure on the threshold. This is the special situation of the only child.

The author tries to get hold of some of the qualities of his soul which he thinks are due to his 'onlyness'. And he describes himself with the following words:

> Silent when glad; affectionate, though shy;
> And now his look was most demurely sad;
> And now he laughed aloud, yet none knew why.
> The neighbours stared and sigh'd, yet bless'd the lad;
> Some deem'd him wondrous wise, and some believed
>   him mad.

His memories go far back into his earliest babyhood. 'I remember lying in my high pram and the smell of that pram remains with me yet.' And then he says: 'Early photographs show me as a pale and solemn child; from the beginning I was observant, but silent and reserved.'

A few pages further he confesses:

> I was also an only child, but not a lonely one. My parents probably thought that the little ragamuffins in our neighbourhood were not suitable companions for me, and I know I was often on my own, but I didn't mind that at all. I would be perfectly happy lying back in my pram, looking up at the silk-fringed canopy it had on hot, sunny days. Or I would crawl contentedly round the pavement in front of our step, digging up the thick black dirt between the flagstones. From my pavement-level viewpoint, it was like looking out over a high sea of stone, and discovering an unknown land where I might never be allowed to go, where strange children played and people who were not a bit like those on our side of the street went about their business in queer ways.

This is a perfect description of the ways of an only child. He is kept away from his immediate social environment. He views it from within the gate of his own house and around him the world is strange yet known. He can observe it but he cannot enter it. He takes part in the activities of this world without really partaking. He is not a child that can forget itself; he is an observer who keeps a distance between himself and the world around.

And gradually whilst still a child, he discovers his 'otherness' in comparison to the people around him:

> At my Granny Johnson's house [he was then four years old], I was vividly aware of her household's inextinguishable zest for life and felt sharply the vitality and the charm of these people who could sing and laugh and play and talk the hind leg off a donkey — they were

all so different from myself. I was often puzzled,
wondering why I couldn't be like them.

This is the situation of the only child. He longs to be like the
other people, gay and unconcerned, happy and sad, forthcoming
and retiring; but all this is foreign to him. He stands and stares
into the infinite, being a child of the threshold.

The family-constellation brought it about that his emotional
life remained untrained. There were no brothers and sisters
with whom constant intercourse was possible. There was no
friction, no fight, no quarrel and no fondness. He was an only
little being, watching the world from a high station, remote
from his fellow-men.

James Kirkup sums up this state of existence when he says:

It was at that early age that the pattern of my life and
personality began to appear. I was a lonely child, though I
was not conscious of loneliness; in fact, I preferred to be
on my own. At the same time, I was torn by the desire to
be with other people, to be part of a circle; I loved the
idea of 'being together' with my Whitmanesque intensity.
Yet after 'being together' with my cousins for a while, I
longed to be alone. I couldn't understand myself. It was
the beginning of a conflict that was to distress me for
many years.'

Here is a further straight assessment of the structure of the only
child. It is a lonely child. He longs to be with others, but when
he is, he wants to be alone. This is the ambiguous position of an
only child's emotions: to meet and be one with others, and to
refrain from doing so at the same time. Here the ambivalence of
feelings is clearly apparent.

The only child has no one but his parents; they, however, are
not his equals, and although they give him shelter and comfort,
they are adult people, standing behind and round the child but
not at his side. 'My parents', so writes *Kirkup*, 'were simply large,

kind, beautiful people with whom I felt happy and safe: I did not see them as individuals until several years later, and did not adore one more than the other as I believe some children do.'

From this statement it is obvious that the parents were a haven of warmth and comfort to the child, but they could not provide the social intercourse so necessary for the unfolding of a growing child's emotional life. Another remark bears this up. The little boy used to visit his granny and aunt every Sunday: 'And off I would go to the tram stop, after kissing Granny and Aunt Anna — something I never like doing, for I only liked kissing my mother and father. It was horrible to kiss other people.' Why was it horrible? Because there were no other real people besides his parents. The others were strangers, foreigners from a distant land, a land that the child had not yet entered.

The company of other people was difficult and cumbersome. 'My mother tells me it used to "make her mad" to see me sitting solemnly without saying a word while other children of the same age "talked away twenty to the dozen." Kind strangers who stopped to chat could never get a word out of me.'

And later when he went to school, all this continues. He admits:

> I did not make friends. My silence and reserve caused
> other children — and some of my teachers — to treat me
> as if I were an idiot. They called me a "looney," but I did
> not mind. I detested the playtimes, for I did not like
> games of any kind. The playground, filled with a swarm
> of shrieking, violent children was a place of terror to me.
> I would try to make myself as inconspicuous as possible
> in the semi-darkness of the "shed," a large open shelter at
> one end of the playground.

This again is typical of the only child. The playground is filled with the teeming life of childhood, yet the only child stands in the safety of an open, lonely shed, at the threshold of existence.

Such quotations as these are of great value as they illustrate

29

the real situation of the child in question better than any psychology can do. The ambivalent state of the only child's emotional life becomes so deeply engrained into his whole make-up that it remains with him for the rest of his life.

An only child when grown up will remain in a kind of splendid isolation. He stands somewhat at the verge of existence, unable to step into the fullness of life. Many such lonely children show peculiar neurotic traits of behaviour in later life. By dint of their isolation, they develop strange habits, turning into hermits or eccentrics.

There are various forms of 'Onlyness.' They are as manifold as is the manifoldness of human existence. Yet in all these variations rings the undertone of 'Onlyness.' It is the difficulty to maintain a proper contact with other people and to live a natural life in which the person is only one among the others.

The only child too often expects to be socially recognized and esteemed. He, being unable to be one of many, craves for a special standing and a special place in life. He often assumes an exceptional position and will not be satisfied before he has achieved it.

The only child will often vacillate between too much and too little social contact, because he is usually rather uncertain of his social abilities. In women this shows itself in a certain form of aloofness and a rigid way of dealing with their own children. Many remain unmarried, and if they do marry, the do not fit into their own family life.

All this presents a rather sad picture of the only child, but it is not meant as a kind of warning. These only children must also exist. Their qualities can lead to great achievements and to high fulfilments. By virtue of his exceptional condition, an only child can sometimes reach out for aims unobtainable for others.

One of the greatest of only children was John the Baptist. Being the son of very old parents, he had no brothers and sisters, and very few companions. Yet he grew and became strong in spirit, and he was in the wilderness till the day of his manifestation to Israel' (Luke 1:80).

30

In John the Baptist, some of the highest possibilities of the only child are revealed. But — he is later on imprisoned and returned to his uttermost loneliness. Yet he had seen 'the Spirit descending from heaven like a dove' when he was permitted to baptize the Son of God who is the Only Begotten Son.

The First Child

I

We now turn to the first-born child. In doing so, however, we at once encounter the question: Is not the only child first-born as well? He is indeed a first-born child, but he is very different from all the other first-born children who stand at the top of a smaller or larger row of brothers and sisters. In considering this difference, we already meet some characteristics of the first child.

There are two groups of first-born children: the one comprises all the only ones, the other — those who head their brothers and sisters. There is a deep cleft between these two groups because the only child is a lonely one; the first child one of several others. We can therefore call the first-born child one who is either an only, or a first child, but we must distinguish between the two, although both belong to the wider circle of first-born children.

In ancient times, the first-born child was outstanding among all other children. And still today the first-born son or daughter is of special value to the parents. No other child is expected and awaited with so much joy and reverence. For months, the young parents are filled with a special warmth of sentiments and feelings. To begin with they share a common secret. Step by step they begin to tell it to their relatives and friends: 'A child is coming.' They feel as were they surrounded by glory and they bask in the radiance of the descending grace. 'A child will come to us.' With gladness and pride and diligence, preparations are made for the great event. This child, the first to come, is really expected and its entry is prepared like the entry of a prince or a princess.

Awaited with every possible expectation, greeted with bliss and joy, accepted with possessiveness — this is the omen of the first-born child. No other child can share this triumphant entry into earthly life. The second and third may be welcomed, but the radiant glow in the hearts of the parents is diminishing and fading. The event of birth is no longer as outstanding and special an occasion as it was when the first child was born.

In primeval times, the first-born child did not even belong to the parents. It was considered to be the property of the divine being who was the leader of the tribe or clan or people. Most of the first-born children were sacrificed either at the ancient altars or by exposure to the elements. Today we think such customs gruesome and cruel; in fact they were an expression of a pious and reverent attitude towards the godhead.

> In India, down to the beginning of the nineteenth century, the custom of sacrificing a first-born child to the Ganges was common. We are told that among the Hindus the first-born has always held a peculiarly sacred position, especially if born in answer to a vow to parents who have long been without offspring, in which case sacrifice of the child was common in India.
>
> ... In Uganda if the first-born of a chief or any important person is a son, the midwife strangles it and reports that the infant is still-born. This is done to ensure the life of the father; if he has a son born first he will soon die, and the child inherit all he has.
>
> ... The Kutonaqa Indians of British Columbia worship the sun and sacrifice their first-born son to him. When a woman is with child she prays to the sun saying: "I am with child. When it is born I shall offer it to you. Have pity on us.
>
> ... Among the Coast Salish Indians of the same region, the first child is often sacrificed to the sun in order to ensure the health and prosperity of the whole family.[7]

In the last two accounts, the inner meaning of the sacrifice becomes apparent. The first child is sent back to the spiritual world in order to become the protector and guardian of the whole family. He will guide the following children down to earth and will remain their spiritual leader and friend.

Something similar existed among the Semitic peoples and especially among the Jews.

> At Jerusalem in these days [the time of the early prophets] there was a regularly appointed place where parents burned their children, both boys and girls, in honour of Baal or Moloch. It was the valley of Hinnom, just outside the walls of the city, and bore the name of Tophet. The practice is referred to again and again with sorrowful indignation by the prophets.

At this time such procedures were already out of date and therefore meaningless and cruel. They were a relapse into old customs but without any spiritual reality; because to Abraham when he was asked to sacrifice his first-born son, redemption was granted and a ram was put in Isaac's place. From then onwards all these human sacrifices were unnecessary and, therefore, gruesome.

We still carry within us some of these old patterns of former knowledge and belief. They vanished from the realm of our ordinary consciousness; yet they rest in the deeper layers of our minds, in the unconscious realm. From there they direct and influence some of our deeds and thoughts.

II

The special halo that surrounds the first-born child is part of this old pattern that is imprinted into our mental existence. It belongs to the only child as well as to the first child; both are special children, conspicuous by their rank of birth. The only child remains lonely, separated from all other children, a shepherd without a flock, a prince without his court.

The place of the first child is quite different. He was for a time an only child until the day when a baby is presented to him and he is told that this is from now on his companion and near relative. A very characteristic description of this moment is given in Hellen Keller's *Story of my Life*.

> For a long time I regarded my little sister as an intruder. I knew that I ceased to be my mother's only darling and the thought filled me with jealousy. She sat in my mother's lap constantly, where I used to sit and seemed to take up all her care and time.

It takes time before the first child is willing to accept his brother or sister. This depends on the difference in age, on the attitude of the parents, on the general conditions in the home and last but not least, on the temperament and the personality of the child himself.

We know that on many occasions, the second child is not at all accepted by the first. It has to bear outbursts of hatred and jealousy, and often has difficulties in establishing its own proper environment. With a certain amount of tact and insight on the part of the parents, these difficulties can be overcome and are usually outgrown in a short time.

The Swiss poet, Carl Spitteler, who probably wrote the most charming book on childhood memories, *Meine frühesten Erlebnisse,* describes how he did not at all like the arrival of his little brother. He could not care less about him and refused to have anything in common with the little bundle of flesh. But this changed and he says: 'As soon as he was able to stand on his two legs and was thereby fit as a playmate, I accepted him.' And he vividly describes a scene when both were put into a bathtub on a hot summer's day and enjoyed the cool element with common joy and gusto, 'no quarrel, no grudge for space, just the opposite; we shouted, splashed and plunged to our heart's delight, peacefully joining our forces.'

Altogether the impact of this first meeting between the first-born and the second child, although occupying an important place in the development of the child, is highly exaggerated in the opinion of present day psychology. The two little rivals will easily find one another if they experience their parents' determination not to give preference to one of them. Here however, the father and especially the mother will have to be highly conscious of what they do and feel. To regard the first-born as well as the second child with equal care and tenderness and to give to each equal parental guidance will make all the difference to the over-coming of the initial difficulties.

These arduous moments in child-rearing are very exacting to parents as well as to their children. And they are more difficult for the first-born than for the other children. The first child begins to realize that his 'place in the sun' is endangered by someone whom he has so far never met. Suddenly there is another child living side by side, sharing his room, his house, the trusted background of the parents. Whence did this being come?

To the second child the shock is sometimes even greater. It meant to come and join the parents — his father and mother; and all at once he discovers a third person who is already occu-pying the place that should be his.

Here two quite different attitudes develop; the first child has to defend his conquered place, the second child has to conquer that which is being defended by another. Their positions are uniquely different and it is this dissimilarity that shapes their social character for good.

The first child is a defender; a defender of faith, a defender of tradition, a defender of the family. The first child preserves the past against the onrush of any new ideas and actions. He has to maintain what has been achieved. The first child has to stand up for what is past whether he likes it or not. It would be interesting to find out how many first children there are in the ranks of judges, lawyers and advocates. They are probably by far in the majority compared to second- and third-born children. There where law and order, tradition and continuity are needed, the first child has his place. It is the first child who is heir to the crown, the title, the leadership of the family, to the inheritance, be it spiritual or material. All these tasks and possessions are laid into his hands and onto his shoulders, because from earliest childhood on, he has been trained in the attitude of defence and steadfastness.

Thus the first child has a unique position in life and in the family. The more brothers and sisters that are born, the more obvious his position becomes. He is a link between the parents on the one hand, and his brothers and sisters on the other. A link, however, can be a bridge or it can be a barrier; like a gate that is either shut or open. These are the two characteristics of a first child. He can either bar the way or bridge the past and the future. He has two faces — one is turned to his parents who represent the past; the other looks on to his brothers and sisters, thereby gazing into the future. The position of the first child has a most important function in the whole flow of the river of life.

III

Some interesting proofs for our observation come from special statistical surveys. It is an established fact that among first children, there is a higher percentage of boys, and that this percentage is gradually lowered towards the third child. With the fourth it starts to rise again.

Should we express this relation in the form of the so-called sex-ratio, we find the appropriate numbers on the following Table. The sex-ratio shows the number of males accounted for to 100 females. 'A sex-ratio of 100 denotes equality. All over the world boys are usually born in larger numbers than girls. In most civilized countries, the ratio at birth is about 105.'[8] This ratio is far exceeded by first-born children.

Birth Rank	New Zealand	Who's Who in America	New England (1)	New England (2)
1st child ...	108 7	111.2	129.0	115.5
2nd child...	105.4	104.2	109.8	116.2
3rd child...	104.1	101.7	103.5	113.0
4th child...	104.4	113.4	124.5	

(1) All families with four or more children.
(2) All families with one to three children.

It appears to be very indicative that a greater percentage of men are entrusted with the task of the first-born child. It is the attitude of the man to be a defender and therefore the sex-ratio among first-born is a particularly high one.

There is, however, yet another interesting and characteristic quality pertaining to the first rank of birth. If not only the intelligence quotient is accepted as a measure of human ability but also men's achievements in the course of their careers, a clear indication for the rank of birth is given.

Mr. Ziegler has picked out from genealogical books some 1210 persons whose records indicate achievement and character above that of the average in Who's Who. He has tabulated them according to both, birth rank and size of family. This gives a fairly clear picture of the extent to which the leadership of America has come from families of various sizes and from persons of various birth ranks within these families.[9]

The following Table shows the respective numbers, indicating the leading part played by those first in the rank of birth.

Birth Rank*		1	2	3	4	5	6	7	Total
SIZE OF FAMILY	1	46							46
	2	59	33						92
	3	73	35	32					140
	4	53	34	47	28				170
	5	42	34	22	24	18			141
	6	27	15	24	21	20	19		126
	7	25	18	18	22	14	14	23	134
		326	177	143	95	52	33	23	849

Here it becomes quite obvious that in every size of family the first child ranks highest in achievement. Especially in the smaller family, he stands far above his second and third brothers and sisters.

Through such examples, the quality and nature of first children gradually emerges. The first child does not have the aloof nature of the only child. The latter may achieve high positions in life, but inwardly he will always be a hermit, a man craving for companionship but hardly ever achieving it. The first child, equally outstanding, is not a lonely being. He has to be a leading figure, at first among his brothers and sisters and later among his fellow-men. He has a high sense of responsibility and will usually feel accountable for many things that happen around him. He may well develop a great deal of pride and an overbearing attitude in order to comply with the demands of his own high sense of responsibility.

He might get into the habit of ordering his wife and children about and of expecting the wider circle of his family and friends to see in him the person who has to be asked before any decisions are taken. Many first children are filled with bitterness and a sense of deprivation when they are under the

---

* The original table in Huntington's book comprises families up to fifteen children. In order to make things more distinct, I reproduce here only the numbers pertaining to families up to seven children.

impression that not enough regard is paid to the position they have achieved.

There is, however, a constant undertone of guilt connected with their achievements. That is because they had to forgo certain possibilities open to others since their early childhood. The first child has to defend even when he would like to attack; he has to comply even when he thought it wrong to do so. The first child will often obey when he would rather like to revolt. He is the slow but steadily moving vanguard in the developing march of mankind.

There is often a strong and bitter tension in the emotional structure of first children. Many of them are impatient to reach the top of the ladder. This need not be due to a drive for power and to ambition. It can also be due to a great amount of idealistic striving and the longing to reform the world. But against this inner tension stands the innate power of being a first child with the necessity for preserving and defending.

IV

These general characteristics of the first child are somewhat modified and varied by the different patterns of the family constellation to which the child belongs. It is a different thing to be the first of two children, or the first of three or four or even more brothers and sisters. It is likewise a different matter if there is a first brother with one or two sisters to follow, or if a first brother has several more brothers after him.

The larger the number of siblings, the greater the variety of family patterns. In a family of only two children, there are not more than four probabilities: either two boys or two girls, or a boy and a girl, or a girl and a boy. Here are 'only' four possibilities; but how different are such families in their whole structure! What a difference it makes whether a sister has a little brother or a brother is followed by a sister. The various types of his family-texture should always be visualized when studying a man's personality.

In a family of three children, eight different patterns are possible. In families with four children, there are sixteen probabilities of structure. Each one of these constellations imprints itself upon the growing child, and especially upon the first as he is the natural leader of the whole flock and moulded by its growing form.

The family-patterns are like musical motifs or melodies. There is, for instance, the motif of the two sisters; the first soon experiences her obligations towards the younger and reacts accordingly. The older sister often develops an attitude that is not always agreeable. In many a masculine streak appears, overshadowing the girl and the woman in them. These masculine qualities can be of a varied nature. One girl develops a jolly and jovial attitude and forceful habits, behaving more like an emancipated student than an ordinary girl. Another first sister may strive for complete independence and resourcefulness; she will do a lot of smoking although she actually does not like it. It appears as if the first sister of the two acquires masculine habits so as to pose as a brother. Therefore a kind of androgynale quality often appears in this type of first child.

Quite the opposite occurs in first sisters followed by a brother. Their feminine attitude and features are strongly prevalent though again they appear in many different ways. In the one, the motherly side will develop especially; in the other, the desire for support and help will be shown. In most of them, one particular side of womanhood is pronounced, as if the little brother had awakened the feminine character in them already very early on and had thus caused it to be particularly strong.

It is most intriguing to observe such differences once the key to the recognition of them has been found. It is amazing to discover how little attention has so far been given to all these human qualities in their relation to the environment of childhood. Here, as we now learn to understand, lie some of the fundamental causes for the development of our social habits.

A family of three sisters again gives to the first a quite different setting. I have had the opportunity of observing several such families and the first sister always had something in her social conduct that was typical but rather difficult to put into words. Without realizing it, she assumes the appearance of some high-standing lady; a duchess or a Lord Mayor's wife or some such person. They are difficult to approach, they make contact with other people as if through a shell, and only later in life when they grow into their own and perhaps build up a family themselves, do they change to ordinary habits. Did the two little sisters act like courtiers or ladies-in-waiting, and did they provide the background for their 'queen' to react accordingly?

As soon as a brother joins the company, everything seems to change and turn towards normality. With two sisters and one brother, or one brother and one sister, the general characteristics of the first child come to the foreground and do not deviate toward peculiarity and oddity.

The types of reactions of first brothers to their family patterns is again quite different. The developing personality is much more self-centred in a boy and he therefore reacts in a different way. If he has to cope with three brothers, the first will need to key up in order to maintain his position as leader and guide. Some boys might pursue special trends in an effort to gain perfection in one or other field of activity. They may train in one particular kind of hobby or sport or learning and thus show their special gifts and qualities.

As soon as a sister or even two sisters enter the ranks of the family, the first son is quite at ease and his social habits are fair.

If on the other hand, there are two or three sisters in his wake and no other brother to keep the scales in balance, the first shows signs of becoming a pasha. It depends on him as to what kind of pasha he will be; either one full of good humour or a rather disagreeable kind of boss.

The first boy with one sister develops qualities of serene behaviour. He may also become as stiff as an old schoolmaster, because he has imagined himself from early days onward as the teacher of his female companion.

With a brother instead of a sister, the first boy becomes self-assured and condescending. From early childhood on, he has had a servant at his side; his younger brother was either his butler or his gamekeeper, his attendant, or his aide-de-camp.

In all these different forms and manners, the social behaviour of first children develops. What we have so often thought to be an innate quality belonging to the individual, now appears as an acquired attitude, shaped by early experiences among brothers and sisters. It will become increasingly necessary and valuable to follow up these indications which I have based on simple observation in a considerable number of cases.

To complete the picture of the first child, we still have to consider another side of his background: the relation to father and mother.

V

In this respect the first child holds a unique position. He is the mediator between his parents and the rest of his brothers and sisters. However carefully and wisely his parents will try to maintain their relation to each one of their children, it will always be the first who bears the full impact of the interplay between parents and children. He is the one whose face is turned both ways: to the parents as the representatives of the past, to his sisters and brothers as the guarantors of the future. He belongs to neither — because to his parents he is the child, to his sisters and brothers he is the substitute for the parents. His position is an ambiguous one. The parents are the captain of the ship of the family; the first-born is the ship's coxswain. He is part of the crew and yet he is not. The older he grows, the firmer must be his grasp on the wheel.

A first child is rarely able to experience the carefree wonder and beauty of childhood. From the start, he is more conscious of everything around him as well as of himself, and thus he loses the natural attitude of the child. All first children are the piers of the bridge over which other men march. This is the special task assigned to first-born children.

At the beginning of Rome when it was still a small settlement around the seven hills at the foot of the Alban Mount, the second of the mystical kings of Rome, Numa Pompilius, is said to have introduced a new godhead to his people. His name was Janus. In the course of Roman history Janus gradually grew in importance and at last became the leading god, overshadowing all others. The first month of the year, Januarius, was called after him as he was the first one. On one of the hills of Rome, the Janiculus (it is still called so today), twelve altars were erected in honour and veneration of Janus-Januarius, indicating that he was the leader of the year with its twelve months.

This god was also the guardian of doors and many of the Roman houses had an image of Janus above the portal. *Frazer* says:

> I conjecture that it may have been customary to set up an
> image or symbol of Janus at the principal door of the
> house in order to place the entrance under the protection
> of the great god. A door thus guarded might be known as
> a 'janus foris,' that is — a Januan door.[10]

The image of this imperial god of the Romans always showed a head with two faces looking in opposite directions; one of them

47

was bearded and appeared to represent a mature, sometimes even an old man. The other face was smooth and youthful in expression. Many such images are known. The bearded face was identified with Saturn and the younger with Janus. It is not known whether Janus was identical with Jupiter. But both, the elder as well as the younger face are the image and the idol of the god who guarded the Roman gates and who began the Roman year.[11]

This double-headed image was not confined to Rome alone. It was also found among the idols of many negro tribes in Africa and South America. It is an image that goes back to primeval times of man's becoming. What does it indicate?

It represents the forces of every first-born child; like the first-born, Janus looks both ways. When he looks into the past, he bears the face of his father, Saturn. When he looks into the future, he bears the face of Jupiter, the son, the first-born one who overpowered all the other gods. Saturn and Jupiter, father and son, are shown as one and the same concurrently. And *that* is the nature and the being of the first child. The first child guards the principal door of the house, because he is the gate between the parents and their children.

Janus heads the twelve months of the year and he was often portrayed holding a stick in one hand and a key in the other. These are the two real attributes of first-born children; they guard and open the gates of man's progress at the same time.

It is understandable that it was just the Romans who worshipped the powerful image of the first-born child as their leading god. Roman history with all its achievements and greatness is the picture of the deeds of the first child. Not the Greeks — the Romans are the first-born children of Europe. Both came from Asia Minor; both hail from Troy. The Roman son is the carrier of external history; the Greek son is the carrier of the inner history of the last centuries before Christ. And it is Janus, the god of the Roman people, who inspired every single 'civis romanus' with the conviction that he was the bearer of the rights to which every first-born man is entitled.

This lasted a few hundred years, until the day when another first child was born. 'When Joseph woke from sleep, he did as the angel of the Lord commanded him; he took his wife, but knew her not until she had borne her first-born son; and he called his name Jesus' (Matt. 1:24f).

A few days later, the Three Kings from the east appeared, having been led by a star to greet the child. They brought their gifts — gold, frankincense and myrrh, to be placed before the newborn Jesus who now becomes the representative of all first-born children.

The time of Janus had come to an end. Thirty years (a Saturnian cycle) after the Three Kings had presented their gifts, the child had grown into manhood. He now stood at the side of John the Baptist at the river Jordan and was baptized. 'And when Jesus was baptized, he went up immediately from the water and behold, the heavens were opened, and he saw the Spirit of God descending like a dove, and alighting on him' (Matt. 3:16).

This happened during the month of Janus — on the 6th of January. It is the eternal Christmas Message to all first-born men. Since this historical moment, they bear in their innermost soul the image of the first Child who suffered so as to become the vessel for the Holy Spirit.

Janus was superseded by Jesus; Januarius by Epiphany. Since then, every man who is willing to follow Christ becomes again a first child. He becomes a pier for mankind's bridge. Since then, all prerogatives of first children are gradually being overcome. But only after many millenia to come will the message of the Jordan be understood: 'Unless one is born anew, he cannot see the kingdom of God' (John 3).

When this comes about, a man will no longer be a first-born on earth. He will be a first-born in the Spirit. This however is open to every human being whether first-born or not.

The Second Child

I

In our endeavour to analyse the social aptitudes of people in connection with their place as children in the framework of their family, we so far encountered the special characteristics of the only child and the first child. We discovered what special traits of behaviour are almost invariably associated with an only child, and that a first child shows equally defined social behaviour patterns. We characterized the latter as a 'defender'; a defender of faith, a defender of tradition, a defender of the family. The first child preserves the past against the onrush of any new ideas and actions.

It is interesting and it should therefore be put on record, that the founder of Individual Psychology, Alfred Adler, who also attempted to investigate the influence of the family-constellation on the psychological development of men, came to somewhat similar conclusions. Phyllis Bottome, one of his close associates describes his findings as follows:

> An 'eldest,' Adler discovered, was generally a dependable, conventional, authoritative, law-abiding child, standing by its parents in its protective and sometimes domineering attitude towards the younger children; but this is by no means invariably the pattern of an eldest — since the child may take what Adler has termed its 'dethronement' by a second child so much to heart that it becomes discouraged, loses all self-reliant powers, and refuses to accept responsibility; but an "eldest" to whom his parents have given a wise and loving explanation of his followers in the family, so that he feels he has an equal stake in their well-being, is unlikely to lose courage or fail to keep his leadership.[12]

In this description, some of the fundamental features of the first child are clearly outlined and come rather near to our own, independently reached conclusions. It is the first proof of the grain of truth in our version of these questions. Adler approaches them from a very different angle. He tries to find the cause for special psychotic and neurotic traits in the make-up of the human character, and was thus led to consider the part played by the family constellation. He did not realize that the growing child is influenced mainly in its *social* habits by its place in the family, and that all other qualities derive from different realms. He ascribed the difference in the various children in one family almost entirely to their placing. This, however, is an overestimation, and discredits all the individual qualities that every human being brings with him when entering the earthly field. I must reiterate that only the *social* habits and no others are determined by the place the child holds in its family-circle.

Individual Psychology also has special ideas about the second child. To quote from the same book:

> The second child, Adler held, is usually a rebel; authority is unlikely to have any charms for him, and he is more likely to egg on his younger brothers and sisters against the 'eldest' and the parents, than to do much conventional governing on his own. The second child is often a shatterer of conventions; a discoverer and a thruster into the unknown. He is, as it were, born 'modern.' He may not have more creative gifts than the other children, but he is spurred on by his desire to overtake the 'eldest' into a more decisive and practical use of the gifts he has. On the other hand, a 'model' eldest may set so high and severe a pace by his dazzling qualities plus his privilege as a first-born, that his second out of sheer despair at coping with such superiority may become either an extremely naughty and difficult child or even run off the rails altogether.

From this description it is obvious that in Individual Psychology, the same fundamental qualities are ascribed to the first as well as to the second child. They are valued with the same measure and the yardstick is their drive for 'the place in the sun'. In Adler's opinion, the second child is the runner-up of the 'eldest', and both are in a race for life and death. Here the devastating influence of Darwin's ideas can be detected. Also for Adler, life is a struggle for the survival of the fittest; a continuous battle, an unending fight which already starts in earliest childhood in the shelter of the family.

As far as my experiences and observations go, the nature of every second child is totally different from that of the first. The second child rarely has the intention of catching up with its elder brother or sister; the second child is not a conqueror and by no means a defender. It is a second child and born into this special place in order to fulfil an entirely different task within the web of mankind's life.

I should like to make this point as clear as possible. The place in the family constellation is not the result of mere chance; just the opposite is the case — for every one of us the rank of birth was chosen according to the plan of life assigned to him by destiny. It is a pre-arranged order that puts one person into the first, and another into the second or third place in the family. These special ranks are meant to mould the social habits of their holders; the inner nature of the individual is wisely prepared to conform with these assignments of destiny.

It is too simple a thought to think that the family is a race course where the various children begin their run on the turf at different times, the eldest having the best chance of winning, with all the others except the second, far behind. No; each child has a different task to fulfil according to its rank. It is our wish here to elucidate the various tendencies so that the higher meaning of each birth-rank can be divined and experienced.

Disharmony comes about when a first child is given the task of a second one, or when a second child upon the death of an elder brother is forced to take his place. Here, often, lie the roots of psychotic and neurotic disorders in the sphere of social behaviour. As long as a third child remains in the third, and a second child in the second rank, all will be well. We should learn to know the task of the second child in order to understand its place in the social order.

The archetypal image for it was laid down in the story of the Creation. The fourth chapter of the Genesis describes the brothers, Cain and Abel; the former being the elder, the latter the younger of the two. Both brought their offerings to the Lord. Abel's sacrifice was accepted, but that of Cain refused. 'And when they were in the field Cain rose up against his brother Abel, and killed him' (Gen. 4:8). In this world-moment of human history, the never-altering tasks of the first and second children were laid bare and open. Every first-born child bears a part of Cain's destiny upon his shoulders. Every second-born shares the fate of Abel in divine acceptance and earthly incongruity. These points are the first for us to comprehend.

II

The Bible describes the first two brothers of all mankind in a very characteristic way. Cain was 'a tiller of the ground'; Abel 'a keeper of sheep'. If we search for the deeper meaning of such statements, we cannot be satisfied with the obvious answer that Cain was a husbandman and Abel a shepherd. The Bible awakens within the reader the archetypal images that lie behind such descriptions. When Cain is referred to as 'a tiller of the ground,' the curse pronounced upon Adam when he was driven out of Paradise resounds in it. 'Cursed is the ground because of you; in toil you shall eat of it all the days of your life; thorns and thistles it shall bring forth to you; and you shalt eat the plants of the field' (Gen. 3:17f). This stern condemnation that accompanied

Adam's departure from the Garden of Eden is handed on to Cain. The latter inherits his father's guilt and has from then onwards to carry it himself. The first-born son becomes the bearer of the curse laid upon his father. He has to work the ground and redeem it by the labour of his hands.

Abel, the shepherd, is of a different nature. He is the friend and companion of his flock; he lives among his beasts and shares their carefree life. We can picture him sitting on the stump of a tree, carving a flute out of a twig and playing a melody of joy and reverence into the silent beauty of the world. His heart and mind are filled with the wonders of this earth. He loves the trees, and follows the passing of the clouds with his gaze.

Cain, walking behind the plough, breaks furrows into the ground. His back is bent and his shoulders laden with the weight of his destiny. His task is to fetter himself ever more to the soil and to connect himself even deeper to the gravity of earth and matter. He is to till and to plough, to dig and to sow, to mine and to hammer, to forge and to transform all matter into shape and function.

Abel is a dreamer; he listens to the voice of his sentiments and feelings. He follows the course of his own thoughts and longs to be back in the realm whence he came. His interest does not lie with the earth and her needs and destiny. His yearning reaches out into the higher spheres of all existence.

Cain is concerned with the transformation of the earth. Abel's task is to overcome the earth. Cain is immersed in the tasks of the present; Abel in listening to the past, continually tries to prepared the future. Here lies the real meaning of the refusal of Cain's offering and the acceptance of Abel's. Cain's place is the earth and the smoke of the offering of his fruits and gifts is turned back to the ground whence it rose. Abel's offering is accepted because his place is not the earth but the Spirit-Land. Cain looks downward to the smoke of his sacrifice; Abel's gaze is turned upwards to the realms where his offering is accepted.

And Cain has to slay Abel so that the curse pronounced upon Adam is fulfilled. Cain is making a further step away from

Paradise; he continues the road his parents have chosen. In Abel he sees his own longing, the yearning every human being has to return to the house of his father. But Cain is the prodigal son who must go out into the world and thus carry out God's command. Cain slays Abel in obedience to God; he is God's child "'If anyone slays Cain, vengeance shall be taken on him seven-fold." And the Lord put a mark on Cain, lest any who came upon him should kill him' (Gen. 4:15).

Every first-born child bears the mark of Cain on his fore-head. He is burdened by Cain's deed, and deep in his uncon-scious, the memory of it is buried. But at times, its restrained power arises and another Abel is killed. We all bear the impact of men's early deeds as hidden attributes in the depths of our exis-tence.

Abel, though slain by his brother, remains his constant com-panion. In every second child, a new Abel grows up; he bears in himself the longing for the Kingdom of God to which he wants to return. Abel is rarely a fighter. He is usually a pioneer, a seeker, a dreamer, a poet, a saint. He is not so concerned with worldly matters. He likes to live without making too much effort. Existence does not only mean sweat and labour; it is joy and bliss, experience and wonder. Abel takes things much easier than Cain. His heart loves the world because it is not such a threat to him as it is to Cain. Abel has a sense of humour and it needs a good amount of disappointment to make him feel embittered, whereas Cain is quickly disturbed and distressed. Cain lives under the spell of duty; life to him is an obligation that has to be honoured in every possible way. The Cain in us disapproves of leisure and bliss, of a free day and of a walk through the fields. The rigid laws of the Plymouth Brothers or the Lutherans or the Calvinists are of Cain's making. The embittered attitude of their founders still casts the shadow of stern duty over their congrega-tions. Their lay-helpers are called 'Elders' because they assume the attitude of the first-born, and thus become the children of Cain. Here appears in exaggeration and often in caricature, what is otherwise one of the main bricks of the house of mankind.

Many quarrels among people would be more readily under-stood if the fighting parties were conscious of the facts described. How often can a teacher who is a first-born child make the life of his second-born pupils a torture! Simply because he expects a sense of duty where it does not exist; he awaits a serious frame of mind where play and joy live instead. Situations continually arise which lead to hatred among people because the Cain and the Abel in them are again fighting one another. And it is always Cain who slays Abel, but the sequel of the deed is a disaster for Cain. Abel suffers, but Cain is tormented. Abel endures the blows, but to receive them is less painful than to deliver them. Cain hurts himself when he strikes Abel, yet cannot help it.

A very typical example of this eternal struggle is the rift between Sigmund Freud and Alfred Adler. They were in close association for almost ten years, but gradually the domineering attitude of Freud who was a first-born child was unable to bear up with the carefree spirit of Adler who was a second son. Cain slew Abel and the latter accepted the blow. Freud in the end was the sufferer. He was never able to transform the bitterness in his mind and to turn it into forgiveness.

III

In the course of the last three years, a simple book has made a deep and lasting impression on numberless people. It is the plain and unassuming story of childhood spent in Battersea, one of the suburbs of London, during the first decade of this cen-tury. For quite a time I had to ask myself where the actual beauty and the enthralling power of the content of this book really lay. *Over the Bridge*[13] is a book full of reason and wonder, of sublime reality and refined objectivity; but this alone does not explain the strong grip it has on the reader. Then I suddenly knew what it was: *Over the Bridge* is the modern story of Adam and Eve and

Cain and Abel. And it was Abel who wrote it, for Richard Church is the second child who retells and relates the experiences and adventures of his childhood. To do justice to the book, I would have to quote it from the first to the last page. Everybody should read it. Nowhere else can so much information be gained about the eternal drama of our forefathers and their deeds within our souls and minds. A clearer image of modern Cain and Abel has perhaps never been painted.

The story opens on the first day of the century with

> ... two little boys walking with extreme care and anxiety across Battersea Bridge at half-past three in the afternoon. Their concern was immediate, for the elder brother, a small fellow of eleven, with a large nose, brown eyes, and a sallow skin that gave him a Spanish cast, was carrying an aquarium. This task so occupied him that his follower, the brother who shadowed his life, and for whom he usually felt solemnly responsible, was for the moment forgotten.

This younger brother was just seven years old and it is through his eyes that we look into all the following events. He was quite different from Jack, the older boy. Jack 'was the one who looked ahead and liked things to be in proportion and complete. That may be why he walked with such grave attention to his footsteps, head bent and deliberate of mien.' The younger boy was shy, somewhat remote and tender, and he liked to chatter when no strangers were present.

This younger boy was overshadowed by a strange disease which attacked him in bouts time and again. For a long period, the attacks occurred on Sunday evenings, and the first chapter of the book closes with the onset of this sickness. He describes it as 'a familiar pain that seized me from time to time, gripping me with tongs in the small of the back, and twisting the tongs until they drew all my stomach into a knot of writhing agony.' I mention these periodic attacks for they are typical of second children. They can occur in many different forms and in various parts of the body, in all kinds of disguises. There can be an attack of asthma, a fainting fit, a sudden bout of diarrhoea or even repeated sore throats.

It is the typical form of reaction of second children to the overpowering might of their environment. They succumb to too strong an impact, as Abel succumbed to the onrush of Cain. The slaying of Abel repeats itself in the periodic physical suffering of second children. The only help during such attacks is the comforting hand of the mother.

> Shivering after this bout and shaken by the friendly old enemy in my swollen stomach, I clung to Mother and would not let her go. But Jack was hovering behind her, dour and anxious, and he was dispatched to heat up another flat-iron, and to bring the bottle of eau-de-cologne from the dressing-table in the parental bedroom at the front of the house. Awaiting these aids, Mother sat on the bed and talked to me, while she tried to conjure the pain away by massage.

Now he has achieved it; Mother is here for him and him only, and Jack is his servant and helps to comfort him. The 'friendly old enemy' in the belly has done it and brought it about.

And later on in the same evening, when his brother returns to the bedroom and settles down for the night, he describes him in the following way:

> He might have been a hundred years old, rather than eleven, so serious, so responsible he was, planning ahead, nothing forgotten or neglected. I listened, a silent lieutenant, proud and adoring. But I was also detached, and half ashamed of the fact that I was wondering how he could be so completely given up to these intense preoccupations with things: the aquarium, or the building of an engine, or the making of a sailing boat. I

> thought him a magician: but I did not want to imitate
> him. I was not patient enough to use my hands as he
> used his.

No clearer description could be given of a first and a second child. 'I thought him a magician'; this is what Cain was, and the thousands of millions of first children who followed him. But the second child 'did not want to imitate him', for he was occupied with many other things in life.

Learning was difficult, but dreaming was easy, the powers of fantasy great and sometimes overwhelming.

> My idleness of mind was beginning to show itself and
> had been noticed both at school and at home ... What I
> lacked in intellectual fibre, I made up in nervous
> sensibility. I thought through my skin, as a cat does ...
> Still more abject was my sloth in the matter of figures.
> Belated in mastering letters and words, I was still more
> behind in grasping the significance and relationship of
> numbers ...

This child lived in a world of sentiments and feelings, a fairyland of wonder and beauty.

> When the slant sun of summer evenings struck the
> aquarium, the effect was so overwhelming that I stood
> there almost in tears. Sometimes at night, when the
> gaslight threw a sombre beam into the tank, I was equally
> moved ...

During this time, it was discovered that he was short-sighted, and the correcting spectacles created a new world for the child.

> This made me surmise that the universe which hitherto I
> had seen in a vague mass of colour and blurred shapes

might in actuality be much more concise and defined. In this new world, sound as well as sight was changed. It took on hardness and definition, forcing itself upon my hearing, so that I was besieged simultaneously through the eye and through the ear. How willingly I surrendered!

And then something of great significance happened to little Abel: immediately after he began wearing his spectacles, he went out with his parents late in the evening, and for the first time in his life, he beheld the stars —

clear pin-points of light, diamond-hard, standing not upon a velvet surface, but floating in space, some near, some far, in awe-striking perspective that came as a revelation to my newly educated eyes. I felt myself swept up into that traffic of the night sky. I floated away and might have disappeared into space had not a cry recalled me. It was my Mother's voice, in alarm, for she had looked around, perhaps impatiently, to urge me along, only to see me lying on my back on the pavement, in a state of semi-coma.

Now Abel had found his home; the starry sky appeared to him and he was so overcome by the new discovery that he fainted under its blissful impact. From then on he quickly learned to read, and he immersed himself in all manner of books. 'It is an understatement to say that I began to read. I stepped into another life.' And later on when he attended a boys' school, he remarks:

Only in reading did I find serenity and self-confidence. As soon as I put down my book and took off the armour of words, I felt the winds of life blow cold upon my nakedness and I shivered with apprehension.

This child, a real son of Abel, experienced in the sordid environment of a convalescent home where he was sent to be cured of
his stomach-attacks:

> ... that time and space were deceivers, openly
> contradicting each other and at best offering a
> compromise in place of a law ... On that winter
> morning, I stood transfigured, with that astounding
> companion, the Jesus whom I had fashioned from my
> reading in the Bible; there I stood and turned to him
> with an eagerness to impart my finding, to share the
> significance, the richness of it.

He, having recognized this, is able to lift himself above the
ground by sheer will-power and to 'glide about the room some
twelve or eighteen inches above the parquet floor.'

This potentially remains with him throughout childhood
and youth. He has power over the drag of the earth; he can
overcome gravity and he lives, a companion of many and varied spiritual forces. And he knows of the gift that was given to
him:

> I was half ashamed of it, as though it were something I
> had stolen, just as later, when I began to practise verse,
> and found myself being seized by phrases not of my
> conscious making, I set the words down in shame. Yet in
> both aspects of flight, physical and verbal, I revelled in the
> wrong-doing, having a remote conviction of faith that the
> obligation was put upon me by a more ancient command,
> perhaps at the beckoning of the hand that scattered the
> largesses of autumnal gold from the elm-tops.

This 'ancient command' endows every second child with special spiritual powers that are his by inheritance. He is nearer
to the Kingdom of God than any other person on earth. It is
his prerogative, but it is also his danger. It can elate him, but it

can also spoil him and make him a fraud and a charlatan. To be a second child mostly means to walk along a rope stretched between heaven and earth; to maintain the balance between above and below is the chief attribute of the second child.

IV

It would be fascinating to now begin to describe the different variations of this eternal pair of brothers. Throughout the history of men, they make their appearance and belong to the most common and known sets of human grouping. We need only to remember the brothers Wilhelm and Alexander von Humboldt; the elder being a statesman, linguist, educationalist and Greek scholar — the founder of the Berlin University, the friend of Goethe and one of the most remarkable participants of the famous Vienna Congress in 1814. His brother, on the other hand, was one of the most successful explorers and travellers of his time, a botanist and geologist of the highest order. To read the story of their lives is to read another modern tale of Cain and Abel.

There are, for instance, the two brothers, Hauptmann, both very gifted poets. But Carl, the elder, is overshadowed step by step by the fame and success of his brother, Gerhard, and at last he dies, embittered and in a state of deep despair. Another tragic example of the failure of Cain we see in the brothers, Hans and Walter von Molo. Here too, we encounter a pair of gifted writers, but the younger outshines the elder and within a few years, Hans withdraws into a form of schizophrenia. He lives in the isolation of a mental hospital until, along with tens of thousands of others, he is 'mercifully' extinguished under the abominable strife of the Nazi regime against insanity.

The character of the second son changes slightly when the preceding child is a girl. Then Abel's anyhow somewhat feminine qualities grow rather more pronounced and he may become a weak and sloppy person. On the other hand, if the distance between him and his sister is not too great, he may acquire some of the characteristics of the first-born son, taking over from his sister the task of being the elder. This is usually not to the advantage of either. The sister becomes a dependent woman without much personality, and the boy is often veiled in his own glory he being a second and a first child at the same time. Something similar happens when a first-born brother dies, and the second one is required to step into his shoes. An air of unreal splendour surrounds him and makes it difficult to bring the true being in him to birth. Such people act as if they were Cain, but in truth they are Abel, and life is for them a more or less continual tension between their real and their acquired selves.

The story of Esau and Jacob is a remarkable introduction into the interplay between first and second brothers. Esau is the representative of ancient man — 'his body like a hairy mantle' and he is given up to the deeds of the earth. Jacob is 'a quiet man, dwelling in tents' and points to the future (Gen. 25: 25, 27). He developed his thinking abilities and was able to wrest the birthright from the first-born Esau. The entire later life of Jacob was the result of his double existence; being the second child with the tasks of the first.

What about Abel's feminine counterpart? Can we find an archetypal image for the second child when it is a girl? She wears the mantle of the perfect sister. She has something in her being and in her social attitude which reveals the eternal image of sisterly existence. She is neither the wife nor the mother; she is first and foremost, the sister, the companion of men and women, the friend and attendant.

She mostly remains in the background. She has no intention of appearing, of shining, of displaying herself and her qualities. This may not always be due to modesty or bashfulness; the second sister can be a rather forceful personality, but usually behind and not in front of the curtain. From behind she can pull the strings and guide those who live in her environment. She can easily grow into a tyrant of modesty and withdrawal. Her attitude of 'downing tools' is often apparent. This force of non-aggression in her is much more powerful than any direct attack or defence would be.

In the background of every community, in the smaller and wider circles of the family, wherever aggregations of men live together, in factories and in offices, in congregations and all kinds of societies, second sisters in all their variations have their special place. Forceful and lenient, devoted and tyrannical, they appear in all forms of disguise. But always and at every time, they represent the eternal sister, the woman who is the companion, not the wife or the mother of man.

Behind these female second children appears an image such as the one we discovered for the second brothers. It is Artemis, the twin-sister of Apollo. In one of the most beautiful books dealing with the gods of the Greeks, *Les Dieux de la Grèce* by André Bonnard, the goddess is described in the following way:

> She pleases herself to range through the forests and to rove over the mountain ridges, swept by the winds; she pleases herself in the company of animals not tamed by men.
>
> Hers are the games of childhood, the chaste and the modest thoughts of adolescence. Beautiful and shy as the beasts of the forest, is she the untamed virgin.
>
> She is pure and cool like the light of the moon which shows to the hunter the path through the thicket.
>
> Gentle or cruel, her arrow reaches its aim safely.
>
> She is the goddess of wild nature, of virgin bodies, of hearts that do not know the passion of love.

These words describe the inner being of Artemis and in this image live some of the fundamental qualities of the female second child. But Artemis had many varied faces; her worship extended over the whole of the Near East and along the shores of southern Europe. In hundreds of temples, she displayed the various sides of her being and the differences of her manifold countenance.

The same differences can be observed in female second children the core of whose personalities are artemesian. Artemis was foremost a sister; her brother, Apollo, was her master and without serving him, she was his companion. Therefore, the most obvious expression of Artemis is found in girls who are preceded by a brother. If the first, however, is a sister, second sisters will show signs of going in the direction of cool and frigid women. They easily turn into schoolmistresses and real spinsters if they are not helped from early youth onwards to overcome their stiffness.

But these are the possible aberrations. In many second sisters a spiritual, sometimes even an angelic determination is present. They are devoted nurses, teachers, doctors and social workers — always playing the second fiddle, yet indispensable in their deeds and achievements to the community of men.

In Abel there is an intimate connection with the world of the spirit. In Artemis, the same quality creates a union with the wonders and beauty of all existence. Abel is the representative of the spirit in man; Artemis, the constant proclaimer of man's soul. Neither Abel nor Artemis are weekday beings; they belong rather to the festival days, to the special occasions, to the outstanding events. The drudgery of life is foreign to them; they will accept it if their help is needed and their labour valued. They keep an unbroken bond with the land whence they descended at birth. First-born children are the true and rightful inhabitants of this earth. Second children are guests — to them the earth is but a temporary place of accommodation.

V

In the previous chapter, we described first children as 'the piers of the bridge over which other men march.' If we transform this picture and speak of a temple in which mankind worships, then all first children are continually at work, building the foundations of this temple. It rests upon their labour, upon their suffering and their intense intercourse with the needs of the earth. Second children provide the pillars and the architraves of the temple. They stand on the foundations their first brothers and sisters provide. They themselves reach upwards and support the roof as the imprint of the heavens, the vault above us. In this way, we can understand the difference in the task and destiny of first and second children, but also see the co-operation and integration between these two groups of men. They do not only need each other; they are necessary for the building of the temple of mankind.

Only gradually are these differences coming to the light of our consciousness in the course of history. But they constitute a knowledge that is of great importance, especially for our present time. During the past forty years, since the First World War, the structure of the family, the building-stone of human society, has been fast disintegrating. Its framework is attacked from within as well as from without. Like other old forms, it is crumbling down, and this shelter of childhood, this haven of moral certainty, is in the process of decay.

Is this a necessary process? Is it an old form that undergoes the natural process of dissolution? Or is it just a temporary re-arrangement such as that of the caterpillar when it dissolves within the chrysalis to be reshaped and transformed into the imago?

Many things which have so far functioned unquestionably have ceased doing so. This is especially true in all spheres of human society. The interplay between parents and children, between brothers and sisters, between master and servant, employer and employee, have ceased working. The machinery of human life in the social field is grinding heavily and almost coming to a standstill. Everywhere there are paid and voluntary helpers who try to keep it going, but it becomes worse instead of better.

Social workers, psychiatric social workers, youth leaders, marriage counsels, public assistance workers, probation officers, mental health assistances, medical officers, health clinics, health visitors, and many, many more — a virtual army of devoted servants working under the banner of help and love — try to keep the social machinery going with the oilcans which are at their disposal. But in quiet moments of reflection, each one of them will ask: For how long is it still going to work?

What has so far moved instinctively, now increasingly becomes a matter of conscious insight and understanding. Millions of people will have to learn anew the deeper significance of being a father, a mother, of establishing a family, of caring for their children, and of communicating with their neighbours.

The meaning of the order of birth belongs to this programme of making conscious what has so far worked instinctively. It is not a question for dry psychologists nor psychoanalysts. It is also not a question for students of the social sciences or for statisticians, although more facts pertaining to this field should be accumulated than has hitherto been the case. The order of birth and its deeper significance is the concern of the students of *human* science. The fabric and the morphology of the structure of mankind has to be studied as a whole if an understanding for the rank of birth in the family is to be achieved. To be a first-born or an only child, a second or a third one, implies tasks which accompany the human being from his birth to his death.

It is not quite correct to state that we are all born equal. We are not, because we are born with different ranks in the order of birth. And whether we bear the destiny of Cain or of Abel, of Janus or of Artemis, makes a great deal of difference on the road of life. More and more, all this will need a new understanding and fresh insight.

The Third Child

I

It appears to be obvious that every human being apart from belonging to the order of human beings and being either male or female, has a third attribute which he acquires at birth: his rank in the family constellation. It influences every man in a very decisive way and plays a great part in preparing him for the task he is to fulfil on earth.

Whether we are born as a male or a female is of fundamental importance for the whole trend of our existence. We know this very well and are forced to arrange our lives accordingly. The division into the two sexes is such a foregone conclusion that we take it as the most natural partition of which we know. It also divides the kingdoms of nature in as far as plants and animals are concerned. In fact there is no walk of life, no pattern of behaviour, no organic form which does not bear the mark of this differentiation.

The order of birth is another motive of great influence in the destiny of man. It does not permeate the whole being in so deep a way as does the differentiation into male or female. So far we do not know of differences in the physical structure of first, second and third children. Nevertheless, the structure of our emotions, the course of our reactions are significantly changed by these facts of the family constellation.

It would therefore be of great interest to have a first idea of the relative percentage of the different numbers of first, second and so on — children. Such numbers will vary considerably in the different types of people from which they are taken. A town population will probably show some differences from a village community. In rural Italy, the numbers will vary from those taken in Stockholm or Copenhagen, not to speak of primitive societies such as people in Africa or Indonesia who still lie in tribal orders.

Nevertheless, a first conception of the various numbers might be gained if we take a mixed group of children attending school. I have chosen such a group. It consists of 264 children between five and eighteen years of age attending a school in a town in Germany. It is a co-educational school and there are 128 girls and 136 boys. Their distribution in the rank of birth is given in the following table:

Rank of Birth	Only	First	Second	Third	Fourth	Fifth	Sixth	Seventh	Eighth
Male	18	36	43	17	16	5	1	—	—
Female	24	29	36	24	10	3	1	—	1
Total	42	65	79	41	26	8	2	—	1

To look at such numbers is very revealing. First of all it shows that first and second children are by far the most numerous. With 54% they comprise more than half of the whole number. This was to be expected; but it is rather astonishing to find that there are more second than first children. We would think that there ought to be more first than second born. It appears, however, not to be so. Naturally, each second child must have a first one as it would otherwise not be the second. Therefore, some of the first children had probably already left school or were attending a different one. However, the peak in the rank of birth at least in our group, is held by the first and second children.

It is further very interesting that the number of only and third children corresponds almost exactly. In our group are 42 only and 41 third children. Of still greater significance is their sex-distribution: because there are remarkably more only girls than only boys, and a similar difference appears among third children. In both groups the relation of girls and boys is 57% to

43%, whereas in the first and second-born, this proportion is almost reversed.

In the fourth children the numbers decrease considerably, and from the fifth- and sixth-born onward, the percentage is quite insignificant. We have thus an initial survey as to how the rank of birth is numerically distributed in a mixed town-population on the Continent.

Among a selected group of adult people which consists of 38 men and 68 women, I found 36 first and 30 second-born. Here again these two ranks are more than half of all the others together. In the same group, there are 15 only and 19 third children, and the small remainder of six is distributed over the rest of the ranks. Here once more, the third and only born are almost equal in number as well as in their sex-distribution.

We can, therefore, say generally that more than half of the present population consists of first and second-born people. About a third comprises third-born and only children in equal distribution. The remainder — not more than one sixth — belongs to all other ranks of birth.

With a certain amount of caution we may state that among every 120 people, we can roughly expect to find:

20 only children
32 first-born
32 second-born
20 third-born
8 fourth-born and
8 who belong to all the following ranks of birth

From this survey, the domineering position of the first two places of birth can be seen very clearly. As all only children hold the first rank, we have 52 first-born, 32 second and 20 third-born, and the small remainder distributed over the other places. This gives the fundamental structure of the social aptitudes of man.

We have so far described the first and second places in this order, and now have to consider the nature of the third child.

II

From our survey, we saw clearly that numerically the third child corresponds to the only one. In character and social bearing, the third child is at least as problematical as the only child. Not only numerically, but in every other way is there a gap between the first and second children on the one hand, and the third on the other. The first child and the second belong together however different they may be. Their destinies are intimately connected, and their sympathies and antipathies are dove-tailed into one another.

The third child appears as an outsider. The first two have begun to accept one another and to share their lives, when suddenly a stranger arrives and gradually makes his way into their common existence. Now a single one stands against two. The first two have grown to know each other during a considerable time; they have learned to get along and to regard each other as given facts. And suddenly a new-comer approaches! It is quite natural that the first two stand up against the third.

From his start in life onwards, the third child is a stranger. There is first of all the rather far away sphere of the parents. Then follows the other layer occupied by the first two siblings, and at last there is the third, the lonely child. His position assumes special significance if several years have elapsed between the births of the second and third child. But even if there are only two years between, the stamp of being an outsider marks the new arrival.

A third child can gradually work its way into the circle of the first two brothers or sisters. It will even put a greater effort into this task and try by every possible means to qualify as a respected partner among his forerunners. If, however, the third is a child with few fighting qualities, it will remain behind and prefer to sulk rather than to conquer.

Here we meet two of the fundamental attitudes of third children. They feel apart, sometimes even cut off from all other people. This separation, however, is a very different one from that met with in the only child. The latter always shows a degree of aloofness. He is above all other people; a first-born with all its qualities. The loneliness of the third child has a different flavour. It bears the sting of inferiority. The child longs to take its place among other people, yet it lives under the firm impression that the others are not concerned with its existence and do not care to make its acquaintance.

Many people suffer from this feeling of inferiority, but in them it comes and goes. In a third child, it is the fundamental layer of its social behaviour. From his early days onwards, he finds himself in an awkward position; he is a member of the family circle and yet he is not. He is within as well as without. He longs to be one of the others and can never fully achieve it.

It is understandable that such a position gives rise to the very complex nature of all third children. A good amount of distrust towards all other people grows in them. They feel neglected or rejected, and their reaction can be twofold. They either withdraw into their own being and build a fence or even a wall against the hostile world, or they gather their strength together and after having done so, break out and try to conquer by force that which otherwise would not yield to them.

Some of the great saints are to be found among third children and on the other hand, both adventurers and bold soldiers. A personality like Ignatius Loyola, the founder of the Jesuit Order who to begin with was a valiant officer in the Spanish army could easily have been a third child.

Another very typical third child was the Crown Prince of the former Austro-Hungarian Monarchy, the Archduke Rudolph of Hapsburg. Two sisters proceeded him and then in 1858 he was born. He had a very unhappy childhood under the rigid rules of the Hapsburg Dynasty. He was a precocious child who was eager to please and to make as many friends as possible. The austerity of his father, Franz Joseph, and the extravagant life of his mother, Elizabeth, drove him step by step into a defensive attitude. He was convinced that everybody rejected him and regarded him with contempt.

The new and modern political ideas he laid down in many essays and memoranda were not accepted and his isolation grew. The relation to his wife failed and he finished by committing suicide. He was in love with a young baroness. They decided to terminate their lives; Rudolph first shot his love and several hours later, killed himself.

In many third children such a sudden break in their destinies can occur. A certain number of them die rather young and sometimes suddenly and unexpectedly. Not only loneliness and segregation is around them; they have a much closer relation to the reality of death than a first or second child. Death seems to be nearer to them than it is to other people.

One of the leading statesman of today has a family of three. The first is a daughter who is married and has herself three happy children. The second, a son, married and is an officer in the Navy. The third, again a daughter, was from her early days onward a frail child. She was not able to be educated in a normal way and always looked thin and poorly. At the age of eighteen, she died.

A famous scientist of our days has a family of four. The first three children are daughters; the fourth one who arrived somewhat late, is a son. The first daughter is happily married and has three children. The second is not married. She is a beautiful and independent woman and works in a film studio. The third daughter, frail, bespectacled, was married. Her husband died and she returned to the fold of the family. She is now an assistant to her father. The boy took up his father's career.

I happened to know a family of three daughters. They arrived in intervals of about two years. The first two were closely related during childhood, but the third was to them the 'little one' and often excluded from their play and study. The first one married and although her marriage was a failure, she remained with her husband until his death. She died a few years after him. The second daughter became an artist. She left the family and started an entirely independent life, leaving all traditions and bonds behind her. The third one developed into a rather introspective young girl and died, not yet seventeen years of age. She was the victim of an epidemic disease and was the only one in the family who succumbed to this illness.

There is another family that I remember. The first two children were girls, the third, a son. The first daughter is a very ordinary, traditional person. She is married to a man who is liked by her parents. The second daughter became an independent young woman very early. She studied and is today a leading child-psychologist. The third, the boy, was from early childhood onwards somewhat withdrawn and difficult. As a youth, he joined a revolutionary political party, became involved in a minor terrorist action, and before being arrested, he committed suicide at the age of eighteen.

Another family with three children: the first one was the delight of the parents. She was a very gifted girl who promised a great future. She died of a malignant disease being not yet twenty years old. The second one is a son who had to push himself into the first place and thus suffered under the discrepancy of his position. The third is again a girl. Since birth she is handicapped by a physical defect of one of the sensory organs and remained in the background though she finished her studies in a brilliant way. Her feeling of inferiority is prominent and she is not fully able to participate in life with the whole of her personality.

These are a few typical stories belonging to third children. They describe very clearly the complex nature and the strange destiny connected to this rank of birth.

III

The third child is a person who has the greatest difficulties in achieving his aim. He flowers quickly but also withers away rather rapidly. A third child is often full of a promise that is hardly ever fulfilled. He is a child who reaches out too high and has too short a time to attain his goal.

The great social reformer, Robert Owen, was a third child. (He actually was the sixth in a family of seven, and therefore held the third place.★) His whole life was spent in reaching up to an aim that was too high and his great and grandiose efforts all ended in failure. His great experiment in New Lanark, his community-settlement, New Harmony, in America, the many co-operative social experiments either deteriorated after a few months or even immediately after they had started. Nevertheless, his tremendous efforts were not in vain, because all the seeds he sowed began to grow, though very much later. His reformatory work in education, in the social services, in health insurance and in the co-operative movement — have all developed at last and are living memories of this great philanthropist.

In Robert Owen another special feature of the third child's character appears. He was a man of the future. His visions were true, but the time was not ripe for their realization, and he was not aware of it. Many a time he proclaimed that the millenium would start within a few months' time. He could not believe that his ideas would not revolutionize the country within the course of weeks. This discrepancy between ideal and reality is a deep-seated quality in third children. This contradiction often leads to their disaster.

Another famous third child was St Thérèse of Lisieux. She was the ninth child of her parents and thereby occupied a third

★ See page 85f.

place. All nine were daughters. Four of them died in early infancy and childhood. The other five entered Holy Orders and the last one died when twenty-four years of age as a true saint.About her childhood, St Thérèse says:

> I had a sensitive, affectionate nature, and I might easily
> have squandered my affections on other people if I'd
> found anybody who could appreciate the depth of my
> feelings. I did try, sure enough, to start up friendships
> with girls of my own age, two of them especially. I was
> fond of them both, and they were fond of me, too, as far
> as they were capable of it; but the love bestowed on us by
> our fellow-creatures is so limited, so fickle! It wasn't long
> before I realized how little they understood me.[14]

These are typical emotions of a third child. The loneliness among other people is great; sometimes it is insurmountable. The road to the within is then taken, and either a saint but much more often a deeply dissatisifed personality in bitter conflict with the world is the result.

St Thérèse had a hard struggle to reach the state of inner peace. Her contemptuousness rose up time and again. Once she wrote to her Spiritual Mother:

> No, I turn my back in contempt, and take refuge in Jesus,
> telling Him that I'm ready to defend the doctrine of
> heaven with the last drop of my blood. What does it
> matter that I should catch no glimpse of its beauties here
> on earth, if that will help poor sinners to see them in
> eternity? And, so though it robs me of all enjoyment in
> life, this ordeal God has sent me, I can still tell Him that
> everything He does is delightful to me.

In these words the inner effort to overcome the nature of the third-born reveals itself. The battle of the mind not to accept a negative attitude but to change it into a virtue. 'What does it matter that I should catch no glimpse of its beauties here on earth!' she cries and knows well in the depths of her being how she longs for this beauty.

Another third child born under totally different circumstances, but rather similar is the youngest sister of the famous violinist, Yehudi Menuhin.[15] He was born as the first child; four years later in 1920, his sister Hephzibah arrived, and in the following year, a second sister Yalta, the third child, was born. All her childhood, Yalta tried to catch up with the two older ones. A typical scene is reported: when Yehudi was eight years old, he went for further violin lessons to New York with his mother and his two sisters. A friend of the family came to the station and 'taking the boy out of earshot, he urged him to be kind to Yalta, for he had noticed a tendency on his part to "gang up" with Hephzibah against her little sister.' This is the typical destiny of a third child.

Not only was Yehudi a prodigy; his two sisters were very talented pianists, especially Hephzibah. 'Little Yalta held her ground with the two older children even if her efforts were somewhat unorthodox; what she lacked in accuracy, she more than made up for with histrionic improvizations which both exasperated and delighted Yehudi and Hephzibah.' She plays up in order to enter the ranks of the two first ones.

Another typical scene is the following:

> The luncheon period was reserved for table-talks in which eight-year-old Hephzibah excelled, emerging as the family's leading conversationalist. The least respectful listener was her younger sister, Yalta, who rarely missed a chance for an impish remark ... Every now and then, Yalta would launch a story of her own, improvizing as she went on, often getting bogged down under the weight of contradictory details or tripping over the flow of her words.

Here again something of great significance for a third child is described. Not only that Yalta tries to be as good a story-teller as her older sister; she wants to do it still better and starts to race with her thoughts and words to reach the goal as quickly as possible. As a result of this too great an effort she trips and tumbles and falls. Many of the third-born try to run much too quickly through life and drop down at the wayside, tired and exhausted.

We could continue to quote instance after instance to characterize the third child's being, but it might be more important to form an overall image of its whole existence. It has a very complex nature and we have already seen that it can develop in many different directions. A saint, a hero, a disappointed misanthropist, a pioneer, an artist — all these possibilities are dormant in a third child. It will hardly ever achieve a peaceful and steady life. A third child will never be satisfied with his own achievements, but will strive for more and ever more.

Thereby a motive of the Greek mythology comes to mind. Phaeton, the son of Helios, asks his father to let him drive the sun-chariot for one day around the skies. After long hesitation, Helios agrees and Phaeton mounts the chariot. His strength, however, is not great enough to guide the impetuous sun-horses, and they run off with him, nearing the earth and setting the world aflame. Zeus himself has to interfere to ward off too great a catastrophe and hurls one of his lightning spears which kills Phaeton as he plunges into the river Eridanos.

This is one of the images of a third child's destiny. Too high an aim is sought and the strength is not sufficient to achieve it; a sudden end sets the seal to a noble but tragic life.

There is, however, another image which describes the being of the third-born with equal truth. In Genesis it is said:

> And Adam knew his wife again, and she bore a son and called his name Seth:, for she said, God has appointed for me another child instead of Abel, whom Cain slew. To Seth also a son was born, and he called his name Enosh. At that time men began to call upon the name of the Lord (Gen. 4:25f).

With the third son, Seth, a new story of mankind began. He became the father of all the generations up to Noah who survived the great flood. Cain was the first, Abel the second, and Seth the third. One of the most beautiful of ancient legends tells of Seth of whom nothing more than his name is mentioned in the Bible. The legend tells how Seth, feeling compassion for his old father, Adam, who suffers from a severe illness, goes out to search for the gates of Paradise. He reaches the gate and is granted entry. In Paradise he receives the gift of three seeds taken from the Tree of Life. He bears the precious gift back and when his father dies, Seth buries the seeds under Adam's tongue. Out of Adam's grave a tree begins to grow and out of the wood of the tree the staff of Moses, the pillars of the Solomon's Temple, and at last the Cross of Golgotha were made.

Phaeton and Seth are similar personalities. Phaeton, however, wants to replace his father, Helios, and himself become the driver of the sun chariot. He plunges to his death. Seth, feeling compassion for his father, reaches out for Paradise, but he returns and holds the future of mankind in his hands. He buries the seeds into the ground of tradition, under his father's tongue, and thereby assures the redemption of man.

Phaeton and Seth — both are preparers for the future. The one falls short of his longing, the other achieves his aim by restraining himself. In both, the destiny of the third child is revealed. Phaeton succumbs to it, but Seth by overcoming himself, overcomes his own fate.

IV

With the description of the third-born child we have come to the end of our deliberations on the order of birth. There are no more than the four fundamental types of children: the only one, the first-born, the second and the third. Just as the only child is a branch of the first, so does the third have a similar offshoot — it is the last child, the late-born straggler who often assumes a special place in the family constellation. He easily grows into a little darling who is coddled and pampered by everybody and thereby spoiled for the rest of his life. But he can also transform his destiny and become Tom Thumb and conquer a part of the world.

A fourth child is the lesser edition of the first, and a fifth and sixth are again like a second and third child. Thus the following order gives the fundamental pattern for the family constellation:

Only child	First	Second	Third	
	Fourth	Fifth	Sixth	
	Seventh	Eighth	Ninth	
		and so on		last child

In this diagram, the order of birth for every further child is clearly marked. It is important to know that from the fourth child on, the fundamental features of the first three sons and daughters are simply repeated. A fourth child is as traditional as a first; a fifth as unconcerned as a second, and a sixth or ninth bears the mark of a third child in every possible respect.

In these later children, however, the features are not as clearly outlined as they are in the first three. The destinies of later sons and daughters are altogether not as conspicuous and clear as the fates of the first three. The latter play the main parts on the stage of life and the others remain more in the background. They are the mutes and members of the choir, not the soloists.

Sometimes, however, one of them defies this rule and rises to the highest ranks of human achievement. So Wolfgang Amadeus Mozart was the seventh child and Thérèse of Lisieux the ninth. Emily Jane and Anne Brontë were the fifth and sixth children, but those are rather the exception and not the rule.

These three types of man represent the three archetypal forms of his social destiny. As a first child, he defends the past, as a second, he lives with the present, and he prepares the future as the third. The defender of the past is a ruler. The child of the present is an artist. The preparer of the future is irrational. All three are needed in the great web of human life.

When we return to the image of the temple we described in the last chapter, we remember what we said:

> All first born children are continually at work, building
> the foundations of this temple. It rests upon their labour,
> upon their suffering and their intense intercourse with
> the needs of the earth. Second children provide the
> pillars and the architraves of the temple. They stand on
> the foundations their first brothers and sisters provide.
> They themselves reach upwards and support the roof as
> the imprint of the heavens, the vault above us.

And the third children? What is left to them? They are the slaters! Between heaven and earth they work and help to cover the temple's vault. It is a lofty job to be a third child and a very dangerous one. Therefore so many of them perish before they have ever reached their aim. What would we do without slaters? Without the irrationalists who see the future in such a way as if it were the present?

Praise be to the destiny of first children. They walk in the wake of creation. The image of God the Father is imprinted on their forehead.

Praise be, too, to the task of second children. They keep our life alive; they fill it with joy and beauty and help us to overcome the heaviness of all existence. In their hearts Christ's image is engraved.

Praise be further to the visions of third children. They prepare our future. They seek for new patterns of existence; they consume themselves for the sake of others. Their hands bear the sign of the Holy Spirit.

Thus every single man, already by virtue of his rank of birth, becomes a labourer in the temple of mankind.

Endnotes

1   Quotations from: *Charles McArthur: Personalities of First and Second Children.* (Psychiatry 19.47. 1956).

2   Mary Stewart: *The Success of the First Born Child.* (London 1962).

3   H. E. Jones: 'Environment and Mental Development' in *Manual of Child Psychology* (New York and London, 1945).

4   J. Jacobi: *The Psychology of C. G. Jung* (London, 1951).

5   C. G. Jung: *Modern Man in Search of a Soul* (London, 1945).

6   James Kirkup: *The Only Child — An Autobiography of Infancy* (London 1957)

7   This and the following quotations are taken from Frazer's *The Dying God.* (London 1936).

8   This and the following quotations as well as the tables are taken from Ellsworth Huntington: *Season of Birth* (New York and London 1938).

9   Ellsworth Huntington (above).

10 Sir James Frazer: *The Magic Art.* Vol II (London 1936).

11 A detailed study of all problems involved can be found in the book by the late Professor Karutz: *Das Rätsel des Janus* (Basle 1927).

12 Phyllis Bottome: *Alfred Adler, Apostle of Freedom* (London 1939).

13 Richard Church: *Over the Bridge* (London 1955).

14 All dates and quotations taken from: *Autobiography of a Saint.* (Translated by Ronald Knox.) London 1958.

15 All quotations taken from: R. Magidoff, *Yehudi Menuhin.* London 1956.

Index

The First Three Years
of the Child

Karl König

The author examines the first three years of the life of the child in relation to the three major achievements of that time: learning to walk, to speak, and to think.

Dr König makes his philosophical approach clear at the outset when he says that one is dealing here with something 'more than instinct, more than adaptation, more than the unfolding of inherited faculties.' These are the three basic faculties that make us human, and their acquisition, König argues, is 'an act of grace' in every child. He goes on to provide a detailed analysis of this extraordinarily complex process.

Floris Books